Life Lessons for My Kids

Mary Walsh

Illustrations by Margarita Aleixo

Discover other books by Mary Walsh

The Curse of Jean Lafitte
Knights of the Corporate Round Table
American Posse
Memories of 9/11
Plenty of Fish in the Ocean State
Once Upon a Time in Chicago
His Second Chance
Wounded but not Dead
Fine Spirits Served Here
You Deserve Better
Where or When
Stable of Studs
Dragon Slayer
Catch a Break

Life Lessons for My Kids

Published by Mary Walsh

marywalshwrites.com

For Adam, Anita, Olivia, & Grayson

My favorite people

Social Graces

Always say "Please" and "Thank You"

When someone offers you something to eat or drink, it's nice to accept it.

Offer the same when someone comes to your home.

Never refuse a breath mint or a piece of gum

Don't let your kids run around in restaurants

Never insult anyone in their home

Give sincere compliments

Watch your mouth

Don't take things that aren't yours

Send gifts for new babies

Call if you will be late

The person in front of you is almost always more important than the one on your cell phone

Be polite

Look people in the eye when you speak to them

Mind your own business

Be a courteous guest in someone else's house - bring something for your host, make the bed that you sleep in, clean your dishes, offer to help

Have good table manners -
don't slouch, chew with your mouth closed, finish chewing before you talk, clean your plate when you're done, put a napkin on your lap

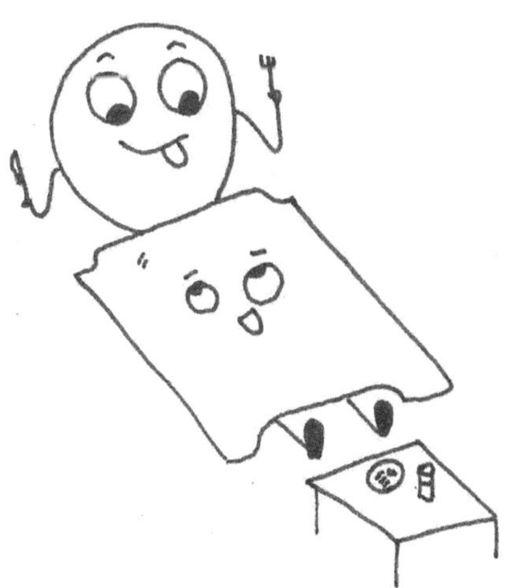

Your Body is a Temple

Take care of yourself

Exercise

Don't smoke or do drugs

Drink in moderation

Practice safe sex

Go to the dentist twice a year

Eat lunch away from your desk

Use sunscreen

Run a Smooth Household

Learn to cook for yourself

Clean up after yourself

Know how to balance your checkbook

Don't keep a monthly balance on your credit card. If you can't pay it off within a month, don't buy it.

Learn how to change a tire

Put things back where you find them

Do your own laundry

Keep receipts - just in case

Pay your bills on time and in full

Keep pens and paper in your car (and napkins!)

Don't buy a car you can't push

Sign your name in blue ink

Put the toilet seat down

Relationships & Family

Kiss your parents and grandparents hello and goodbye

Stay close to your siblings

Be a romantic

It is important to have good friends

Know your family history

Be there for your kids -

go to their functions and pick them up on time

Dress yourself so that you don't embarrass the people you are with

Don't cancel on your friends unless it's a <u>real</u> emergency

Don't marry someone you can live with;
marry someone you can't live without

Get married because you have spent a lot of time with one another; gotten to know one another. Because you are absolutely positive that you are meant to spend the rest of your lives together. You get married because the thought of living without one another is absolutely unbearable.

Get married for these reasons.

Send flowers to your sweetie for no reason

Let your children make their own mistakes so they can learn from them

Own a dog and walk it every day - even in the snow

There are some things you can't compromise on:

a new suit... sure

a dream house... maybe

but the girl (or boy),

you can't compromise on the girl (or boy)!

No matter how successful you become,

you can never completely outrun your past

Know your kids' friends

Flirt

Just when you think you have your parents figured out, they will surprise you

Visit friends in the hospital

Send Christmas cards

Get acquainted with your neighbors

Know that your kids will keep secrets from you

Be a better person than your parents

Know that you can't change someone who doesn't want to change

Have a Little Fun

Don't work so late at night.

There are other things to do besides work.

Experience everything as much as you can

When in doubt, overdress

Travel

Laugh out loud

Go to concerts

Be ecstatic about little things

Dance at weddings and sing in church

Wait tables for a summer

Go to carnivals and street fairs

Try different restaurants -

- and tip well

Laugh, smile, and joke

whenever and wherever you can

Take up a hobby that has nothing to do with your job

Feed your spirit -

meditate, get a massage, write, paint, sing

Socialize with people outside of work - family, friends, and pets!

Laugh at yourself and find out how big of a buffoon you really are

Learn to fish

Never miss, postpone, or cancel vacation time

Save room for dessert

Host parties

Because Nice Matters

Be honest

Don't hide your feelings

Listen to people and accept advice - even if you don't like it or use it

Say you are sorry when you hurt someone

Don't hold a grudge

Remember who you are

Don't be a jerk

Keep your promises

Be modest

Respect others

Have finesse

Play fair

Keep secrets

Never call anyone stupid

Don't sweat the small stuff

Stay calm

Give without expecting in return

Finish what you start

If you think someone could use help, offer before they ask

Volunteer

Be patient

Take responsibility for your actions.

If you screw up, admit your mistake.

Have faith in yourself and others

When you meet someone new, say "How do you do?"
Offer your right hand with a firm handshake.

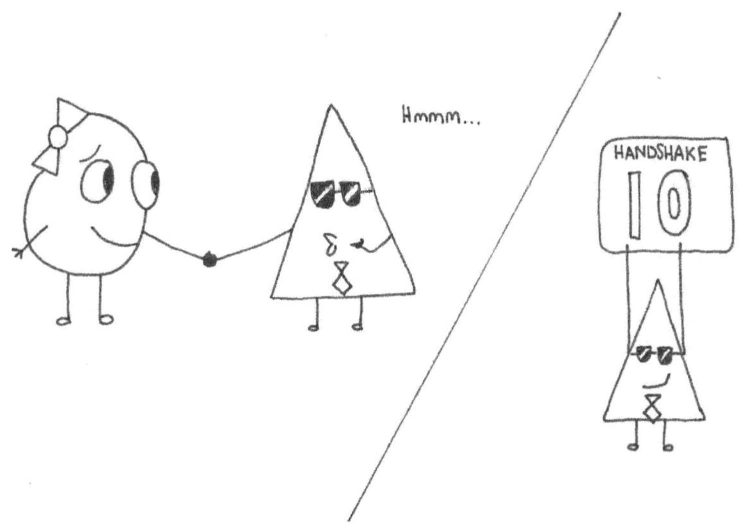

It's okay to be angry;

it's not okay to be cruel

Trust Your Gut

Have no regrets

You can always make more money;
you can never make more time

There are not many idealists in the world because it is a hard thing to be

Take a risk instead of the easy road;

your life will be better for it

There is such a thing as being too cautious

What's the worst that someone can say? "No"

Stand up for yourself and what you believe; fight for what is right

Don't be afraid to be the bad guy in order to prove something is right

When things don't work, improvise

Don't be connected to work 24 hours a day just because you can.

It's not necessary to take your phone everywhere.

It's hard to be brave. It's hard to stand up.

It is, however, the only way.

And finally...

Be Happy!

Thank you for reading my book.
If you enjoyed it, won't you please take a moment to leave me a review at your favorite retailer?
One or two sentences are perfectly fine.
Help an author out.
Thanks!

Want some cool merch from me?
Post a pic of this book on your social media and tag me!
@marywalshwrites

Tag me on:

    BB allauthor

Sign up for my sometimes-monthly newsletter and order autographed books at:
marywalshwrites.com

Follow me on Goodreads and Amazon:

www.goodreads.com/goodreadscommarywalshwrites
www.amazon.com/author/marywalsh2

www.ingramcontent.com/pod-product-compliance
Lightning Source LLC
LaVergne TN
LVHW041225080426
835508LV00011B/1088
9780463894583